Play
Bridge
in 10

minutes

Brian Byfield

Illustrations by Gray Jolliffe

BATSFORD

First published in the United Kingdom in 2011 by
Batsford, 10 Southcombe Street, London W14 0RA

An imprint of Anova Books Company Ltd

ISBN 978 1 84994 016 0   3 1088 1007 2714 6

A CIP catalogue record for this book is available from the
British Library.

18 17 16 15 14 13 12 11
10 9 8 7 6 5 4 3 2 1

Reproduction by Dot Gradations Ltd, UK
Printed and bound by Toppan Leefung
Printers Ltd, China

Cartoons hand coloured, using
the TRIA system by LETRASET
www.letraset.com

*"Got any plans for the
next ten minutes?"*

Since its introduction in the 1920s, Bridge has
become one of the most popular card games in
the world. It's a game for four players, two
playing against two.

Playing Bridge is a chance to socialise, use your brain and enjoy a card game that can be equally rewarding whether winning or losing. Although Bridge is complex, the basic rules are quite easy to learn. So let's get started.

Bridge is played with two packs of 52 cards. Two packs are used so that one can be shuffled while the other is being dealt. Open a pack now. It will be useful as you read the book.

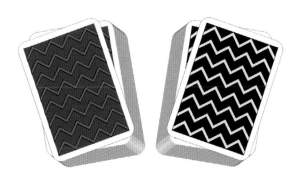

STARTING THE GAME

The pack is spread face down on the table and each player takes a card. The two who draw the highest cards play together against the other two. Partners sit opposite each other. Sometimes husbands, wives and lovers are persuaded not to play together, in case of bickering. Bridge is a game in which egos are easily bruised and, as with driving lessons, couples often make poor partners. So, at the table you should have two opponents and one friend.

"Right - cards, card table - Are you with me so far?"

The player with the highest card deals first, starting with the player to his left. All 52 cards are dealt, each player receiving one card at a time. After the cards have been dealt, the players pick up their cards.

They will have 13 each.

Sorting out your hand

First, sort out your cards. All the Spades together, then the Hearts, Clubs and Diamonds. Now they'll be arranged so they're black, red, black, red, which makes them easier to see and helps you to avoid mistakes.

Then place them so each suit ranks from high to low.

The cards rank from the Ace down to the Two.

Ace, King, Queen and Jack are called Honour Cards. Sometimes the Ten is considered an Honour Card when it's accompanied by the Jack. Spades, Hearts, Diamonds and Clubs are the suits, and rank down in that order. Spades and Hearts are called major suits; Diamonds and Clubs are minor suits.

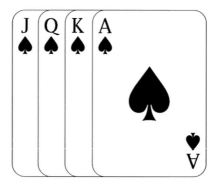

Judging your hand

You do this by counting your points. Here's how it works:

Jack   1 point
Queen   2 points
King   3 points
Ace   4 points

If your hand looks like this, how many points do you have?

The answer is 10 points, an average hand.

As each pack amounts to 40 points, you'll need at least 12 points to make an opening bid. Each pair bids against the other to win the contract. Just like at Sotheby's, the prize goes to the highest bidder.

"Shame he can't play Bridge like he shuffles."

Bidding

The two partnerships bid against each other to decide who will make the contract, which suit will be Trumps, or whether there will be no Trumps. No Trumps is a higher bid than a suit bid.

Trumps

A suit that has been chosen as the master suit is called the Trump suit. If a suit has been led in which you hold no cards, you may use a card from the Trump suit to trump the trick. Trick: four cards, one from each player. The player who plays the higher card wins the 'trick'. If another player does not play a higher Trump card, the trick is yours.

No Trumps

If no master suit has been chosen, all suits are equal.

The dealer always bids first, and bidding then continues round the table clockwise. Each bid must contract to make a greater number of tricks than the previous bid or the same number of tricks in a higher suit. If a player chooses not to

bid he says 'no bid'. If none of the players makes a bid, the hands are thrown in and the cards are re-dealt. The lowest bid is one, a contract to win seven tricks. The highest bid is seven, a contract to win all 13 tricks.

"He's up to his tricks again."

How bidding works

The dealer always bids first, and bidding continues round the table clockwise. The lowest possible bid is 1 Club (a contract to make seven tricks with Clubs as trumps). Then 1 Diamond, 1 Heart, 1 Spade, 1 No Trump, and so on. So the bid above 1 No Trump is 2 Clubs, and so on. A player can only bid a greater number of tricks than the previous bid, or an equal number of tricks in a higher suit or No Trumps.

Bidding is a way of talking to your partner and giving information about your hand. When a player bids he is trying to tell his partner how many tricks, in excess of six, he expects to win. He is also trying to tell him which suit is his strongest, or whether he has a balanced hand.

When a player responds to his partner's bid, he is trying to give him some idea about the shape and strength of his own hand, and whether he can support his chosen suit or give him strength in another suit. Having five or more cards in a suit is a huge advantage. Length is strength.

"I'm bid six diamonds!
Going once... going twice..."

Evaluating tricks

As the first six tricks are taken for granted, only a contract to make seven tricks or more is of interest.

A partnership should hold at least 20 points to make seven tricks.

25/28 points will probably make a game with nine or ten tricks.

36 points or more should be enough to take them all.

Even if you're dealt this hand, try to look on the bright side. At least you'll know it can't get any worse.

PLAYING THE CARDS

The player who wins the contract is called the declarer. The player on the left of the declarer leads the first card. The partner of the declarer then lays down his hand, one suit at a time, face up on the table. Now everyone can see his hand. This is called the Dummy. He takes no further part in the game. The play continues as in all trick-taking games: if a player can, he must follow suit. If he can't, he can trump or discard.

The trick is won by the player who plays the highest card of the suit led, or by the highest Trump. The player who wins the trick plays the next card. If the Dummy hand wins the trick, the next trick is led from there.

Play continues until all 13 tricks have been played. At the end of a game a score is taken. The objective of the game is to win a Rubber. A Rubber is the best of three games.

As in life, it pays to make the most of the hand you are dealt. Don't complain about your cards. We all get bad hands. Remember, playing defence can be very rewarding, especially when you bring down the contract. So winning the contract is not the point. The point is to win the Rubber.

How a game works

In Bridge the players are denoted by the four points of the compass. North plays with South, and East plays with West.

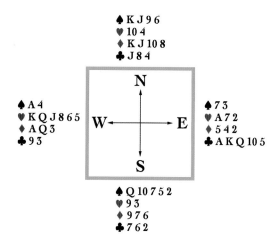

The dealer is North, so he bids first. In this game, he only has nine points, so he says 'no bid'. Moving clockwise, East is next to bid.

He has 13 points, so he opens '1 Club'. South can't bid as he only has two points. He says 'no bid'. West has 16 points and a long suit of Hearts. He knows his partner must have at least 12 points, as he opened the bidding and will have good Clubs.

He now has a chance to tell his partner something else about his hand. Instead of bidding '1 Heart' he bids '2 Hearts', to let his partner know that he has a very powerful hand with strength in Hearts.

North will pass. East will probably take the bid to 3 Hearts, offering some support in Hearts. South will pass and West can then decide whether to bid 4 Hearts. To make 4 Hearts he will have to make at least 10 tricks out of the 13. Can it be done?

Answer: in fact they could have made all 13 tricks, a grand slam, but as a beginner you will have done well to bid 4 Hearts and make the game.

Although West and East hold only 29 points, their hands are stronger because of the 'stopper' Ace in the Spades suit and the length of both Hearts and Clubs.

In fact, whatever card South had led, he couldn't have prevented the Grand Slam.

Sorry, time's up

Well, your 10 minutes are up and you'll have to find some friends, sit around a table and deal the cards. The important thing is to start playing as soon as possible. Scoring, strategies, bidding systems, signals and discards can be picked up along the way. You'll find explanations of some of them on the following pages.

If you do get hooked and want to go on to play in the world championships, have some lessons, join a bridge club and buy a thicker book than this one. Learning to play Bridge well is the work of a lifetime.

Play as much as you can, but be warned. Bridge is addictive. The way to learn is by playing with better players. Don't feel intimidated by playing with people at a higher level.

If you do decide to join a Bridge club, they will welcome you with open arms. They love a convert and always like to see a new face across the table.

"It's been fun, but our game isn't going to improve if we keep playing with you two."

Scoring

When all 13 tricks have been played, the scores are recorded.

WE	THEY
30	
60	120

'We' and 'They' always go at the top. So much nicer than 'Us' and 'Them'. 'We' could be Bob and Carol, 'They' might be Ted and Alice.

On the scoring shown on page 27, in the left-hand column 'We' won the contract with a bid of 2 Spades. In fact, they made 3 Spades, so they scored 60 points below the line and the extra trick is scored above the line. Only below-the-line scores can be counted towards the game.

In the right-hand column, 'They' bid 4 Hearts, winning the contract and the game. So they score 120 points below the line. That's 30 points for each trick: 4 Hearts = 120 points.

In the next game 'They' bid 3 No Trump, which they make, scoring 100 points below the line. That's 40 points for the first trick and 30 points for the other two: 3 No Trump = 100 points. That second game wins the Rubber 2:0, giving them an extra 700 points. Well done, Ted and Alice.

So the final score is 'We' 90 points, 'They' 920 points.

WE	THEY
30	700
60	120
	100
90	920

The main objective is to win a Rubber, the best of three games. A game is nine tricks in No Trump, 10 tricks in Spades or Hearts, 11 tricks in Diamonds or Clubs.

How to work out the score

No Trump:
40 points for the first trick and 30 points for each subsequent trick.

Spades and Hearts:
30 points for each trick.

Diamonds and Clubs:
20 points for each trick.

If you win a Rubber by 2:1, you get 500 points.
If you win a Rubber by 2:0, you get 700 points.

Non-vulnerable:
Small Slam: 500 points
Grand Slam: 1,000 points

Vulnerable:
Small Slam: 750 points
Grand Slam: 1,500 points

When a contract is made, the score for tricks won is entered below the horizontal line. A partnership scoring less than a game in one deal is said to have a part score. Each successful contract is scored below the line. Everything else is scored above the line. You need 100 points or more below the line to win a game in one or more deals.

Once you have won a game you are vulnerable. You'll get higher bonuses if you make a contract, and added penalties if you fail. Being vulnerable does not affect the points for winning contracted tricks. If you score less than a game in one deal you have a part score.

If your opponents then score a game, the part score cannot be carried forward towards the next game. When you win a game, a line is drawn across the score sheet below it, and both partnerships start the next game from a love score. Just like in tennis, 'love' is zero.

"Colin can score.
He works for the Inland Revenue."

Who scores?

Scoring is usually done by the most experienced player, although all the players are expected to keep score once in a while. Some players enjoy scoring, while others would rather leave it to someone else. Accountants, bank managers and auditors can be counted on to step forward.

Overtricks

Tricks that are made over and above the declared contract. For instance, if the contract was 3 No Trump (9 tricks) and 10 tricks were made, that extra trick is an Overtrick. An Overtrick is scored above the line.

Undertricks

When the declarer makes less than the contract. So, if the contract was 4 Hearts (10 tricks) and only 9 tricks were made, that missing trick is an Undertrick. An Undertrick is also scored above the line, but for the opponents.

TRICKS OF THE TRADE

The following section will help you take your game to the next level. It may sound complicated, but don't worry, you won't be on your own. Your partner should be helping you along the way.

Firstly, we cover some conventions that Bridge players use to improve communications between partner.

Blackwood

Devised by Easley Blackwood in 1933. He was the manager of the Metropolitan Life Insurance Company and author of a series of major books on Bridge. It aims to establish whether a partnership holds a Slam (12 tricks) and how to get to the holy grail of Bridge, a Grand Slam, a contract to make all 13 tricks. As you can imagine, this doesn't happen every night of the week. Nevertheless, it's certainly worth knowing.

A Slam bid requires a lot of points between you and your partner: Aces, Kings and a good strong Trump suit. Without the Aces you can lose tricks immediately, so this system is used to ask your partner how many Aces they hold. Before starting bidding Blackwood, you need to know what suit will be Trumps. An 'artificial' bid of 4 No Trumps asks your partner how many Aces they hold. A response of:

5 Clubs says that they have no Aces
5 Diamonds says that they hold 1 Ace
5 Hearts says that they hold 2 Aces
5 Spades says that they have 3 Aces
If they hold all four Aces you probably shouldn't be asking them anyway. But if they do, their response should be '5 Clubs', the same as if they hold no Aces. Don't worry; it's almost impossible to confuse 'no Aces' with '4 Aces'.
If you have all four Aces between you and think a Grand Slam is on the cards you ask your partner for Kings with a bid of 5 No Trumps. Once again, the responses follow the order of suits:

6 Clubs no Kings
6 Diamonds 1 King
6 Hearts 2 Kings
6 Spades 3 Kings

*"I bid six hearts, if
ANYONE is listening..."*

With all this information, the player who started
bidding Blackwood with 4 No Trump can decide
the final contract, and his partner will pass.

With the strength in Trumps and 4 Aces and
Kings, and some careful play, you'll be in with a
fighting chance.

Stayman

A form of bidding introduced by Sam Stayman, an American businessman and Bridge player. Used in response to an opening bid of 1 No Trump to establish a 4/4 fit in a major suit. Its purpose is to find out if the 1 No Trump opening hand has four Hearts or four Spades. On suitable hands, you make an 'artificial' bid of 2 Clubs. It tells your partner you have around 11 points and can cope with all his responses, and that your hand definitely contains four hearts or four spades, or both.

You are asking him if he has four Hearts or four Spades in his hand. If he has four Spades he responds 2 Spades. If he has four Hearts he responds 2 Hearts. If he has neither he responds 2 Diamonds. This is another 'artificial' bid, not a Diamond bid, just a negative response.

Bidding 1 No Trump

To bid 1 No Trump you'll need 12 to 14 points and a balanced hand. 1 No Trump is a popular bid because No Trumps is the game that needs the fewest tricks.

Your partner's response should lead you safely to the final contract.

Responding to a 1 No Trump bid

Your partner opens 1 No Trump. You know he must have 12, 13 or 14 points, no less and no more, no singletons or voids. Your reply is crucial because it is now up to you to decide the contract.

If you have zero to 10 points you know you will have a minimum of 12 points and a maximum of 24 points between you. Even if you have 24 points, there is little chance of making 3 No Trump, so if you have a hand with a balanced distribution you should say 'no bid'. If you have 11 or 12 points, you can start to feel quietly confident. You can now bid 2 No Trumps. This allows your partner to decide whether to go for game with a 3 No Trump bid. If he has 14 points then you will have 25 points between you. If he has 12 points he will pass. With 13 points he will probably take a while to come to a decision. If he has 14 points you'll have a total of 25 or 26 points between you, so it will definitely be a game bid 3 No Trumps.

Turning weakness into strength

Your partner has bid 1 No Trump, promising 12 to 14 points with even distribution.

You hold

♠ 6
♥ J 8 7 5 4 2
♦ 9 6 3 2
♣ J 3

So, you've got two points, but have length in hearts. What do you do?

You can't leave your partner in 1 No Trump. The only option is to play the contract in a single suit contract.

You bid 2 Hearts. Rest assured, he will pass. Remember, length is strength.

This is called a WEAK TAKE OUT.

Take out Double

A Double that is used to ask your partner to bid. East opens 1 Club; you have 1 Club and an equal split in the other three suits. You also have 12 or more points. What can you bid? Difficult, but...

A take out Double guarantees a bid from your partner, because your Double bid has promised him opening points, weakness in the suit bid by East, but a three- or four-card support for the other 3 suits. When your partner bids he takes you out of the Double by bidding his strongest suit of the remaining suits, either 1 Diamond, 1 Heart or 1 Spade. This will ensure a fit and still keep the bidding at a low level. It also puts the brakes on your opponents' ambition.

Making the most of a fit

Your partner has opened 1 Spade. You have four Spades so you know you have an eight-card fit in a major suit. Your job is to tell your partner something about your hand and move the bidding forward. The aim is to maximize the potential of both your and your partner's hand.

Bid A:
'2 Spades'. This shows six to nine points and four supporting Spades. Your partner will only rebid if he has 15 of 16 points.

♠ K 10 5 3
♥ 4
♦ J 9 4 2
♣ K 8 5 2

Bid B:

'3 Spades'. A jump bid showing four card Spades support and 10 to 12 points. It allows your partner to decide whether to make a game bid.

♠ K J 9 3
♥ 6 3
♦ A 7 6 2
♣ K 5 2

Bid C:

'4 Spades'. An immediate game bid. Although you have only 9 points, you now hold 5 Spades. A bid of '4 Spades' tells your partner you have a good fit and strength in another suit.

♠ K J 8 4 3
♥ 8 2
♦ K Q 9 7 4
♣ 6

Always try to give your partner a 'picture' of your hand. If you can 'describe' your hand in the bidding, you should end up with the right contract.

*"Seven Diamonds? If you ask me
that's the sherry bidding."*

TURNING DEFENCE INTO ATTACK

Defence

When defending, try to give your partner as much information about your hand as possible. Try to give the declarer as little information as possible. Whenever possible, always play the cards the declarer knows you hold and keep the cards of which he knows nothing.

Opening Lead

The first card that is played against a contract is always played by the player sitting to the left of the declarer. Your opening lead is very important. It should not be rushed into. This lead can be decisive: one that can bring down a contract or allow it to be made.

Discards: Sending out signals

When a player has no cards of the suit that has been led, they have to play a card from a different suit. Discards can be used in different ways to signal information to your partner. If you like your partner's lead, play the highest card you can afford in that suit. If you dislike his lead, play the lowest card in that suit. Your partner will be watching out for these signals in your discards and will be ready to react to them.

Often your partner will lead an Ace, promising the King to follow. If you hold the Queen or a Doubleton (2 cards) of the suit led, you will want him to play his King and then a third round of the suit. Then you can take the trick with your Queen or trump it. If you hold different cards you will be trying to tell your partner not to lead his King. How do you do this? If you like his lead, play your highest card. If you dislike it, play the lowest card in the suit. This is often called a 'High-Low' signal.

The Penalty Double

Your opponents have bid a contract, which you think they cannot make. What can you do?

You can 'Double' them. If they do make their contract, they get double the points. But if they fail, you get 100 points for the first trick down, 200 points for the second and third trick down and 300 points for each subsequent trick, if they are not vulnerable. If they are vulnerable, you get 200 points for the first trick down and 300 points for each subsequent trick.

Playing Trump cards

Usually the declarer and his partner will hold at least 8 cards of the Trump suit – this is called a fit – leaving the defence with 5 Trumps. If you are the declarer you'll be hoping they'll have a 3–2 split. This allows you to finish off their Trumps in three rounds. You will then have 2 Trumps remaining.

If you play a Trump in your hand to a Trump in Dummy, you will only make one trick. You have to judge whether it will be better to draw your opponents' Trumps quickly or use your Trumps to trump low cards in either hand. Trumps are precious and allow you to control the game. Make the most of them.

The Finesse

You are South and North is the Dummy. You want to win two tricks with your heart suit. If you lead the 4 from your hand, East or West could take it with a nine. If you lead your Queen, the hidden King will take the trick.

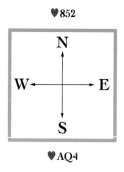

♥852

♥AQ4

If you play the Ace, you will only win one trick because the King will still be waiting for your Queen. So what to do?

You use a trick to win a trick. You can lead any card from Dummy. East plays next. If East has the King and plays low, you 'finesse' the trick with your Queen, which wins the trick.

The problem is, if West has the King he will take your Queen and you can only win one trick with your Ace.

But don't worry; fortune often favours the brave. The important thing is that by attempting the finesse, you gave yourself a chance to make both your Ace and your Queen.

And the good news is that if it comes off, which should be 50 percent of the time, you've squeezed an extra trick from your opponents. It's a no-brainer.

MIND
GAMES

Beginners are often tempted into joining the bidding, especially when their opponents are winning auctions and contracts. Often it is done to try to throw their opponents by making a 'fake' bid. Although this can be effective, it is a risky business and just as likely to confuse your partner. Often, an informative Double is a better way to disrupt your opponents' bidding.

Most top players are skilled at confusing their opponents with an unexpected bid or an intimidating Double.

As a beginner, you'll find that honesty is the best policy.

Try not to be impatient. Your time will come. Playing well against a contract is a vital part of the game. During a lifetime of playing the game you will be playing defence at least 50 per cent of the time.

"My wife ran off with my partner – you don't play Bridge, do you?"

Building a happy partnership

Like a happy marriage, a Bridge partnership is built on public loyalty, forgiveness and trust. So don't roll your eyes when your partner's making a pig's ear of the contract.

"Heads! You get Audrey!"

OTHER THINGS
WORTH KNOWING

Acol

Acol is a bidding system used in British tournament play and widely used in most English-speaking countries, the exception being America, which uses the Standard American Yellow Card.

Acol is a natural system: opening bids, responses and rebids are made with at least four cards in the suit bid. Most No Trump bids are made with balanced hands. It is a four-card major suit system: only four-card suits are required to open 1 Spade or 1 Heart.

Ruff
Playing a trump card when another suit is led.

Void
When you have no cards in a suit.

Singleton
When you hold one card in a suit

Doubleton
When you have two cards of a suit.

Small Slam
A contract to make 12 tricks. If you make it you'll earn a minimum of 500 points.

Grand Slam
A contract to make all 13 tricks. If you make it you'll earn a minimum of 1,000 points – and lots of Brownie points from your partner.

Yarborough

A hand that contains no card above a nine.
Named after the Earl of Yarborough, who used
to offer odds of 1000:1 against it being dealt.
But, as you can see, it's a hand nobody wants.

Variations on a theme

If one of your regular four has gone AWOL, it is possible to play the game with three players. You can find the rules for several versions on the Internet.

"Need a fourth?"

If East has run off with West, and there's just the two of you, there are again several versions, generally known as 'Honeymoon Bridge'.

"The honeymoon is so over!"

f things don't work out and you're left all alone, you'll always find a bridge column in a newspaper or magazine. They are instructive, clear and well worth playing out.

Unlike tennis or squash, the great thing about Bridge is that you will be able to carry on playing when you're old and grey, until that distant time when you can still remember which cards have been played, but can't remember who you're playing with.

Worth remembering

Whether you are the declarer trying to make a contract or playing defence against the contract, remembering what bids have been made and what cards have been played will make you a better player. As there are 13 cards in a suit, if all the players play 3 each, the 13th card will win a trick, even if it's a 2. You'll find, as a hand progresses, that the better players have a knack of knowing not only what cards are left but also who has them.

It's only a game

No matter how good you become, remember that Bridge is just a game. You can enjoy it at all levels and you'll meet complete strangers who, through Bridge, will become friends.

Like golf, Bridge is a game where a lifetime of practice is never enough. Maybe this helps to explain their enduring popularity. However, Bridge will always have the edge because Bridge is played at golf clubs, whereas golf is never played at Bridge clubs.

"It's 9 pm Robert. We're
here to play Bridge."